Power-Filled Words That Change Lives

by
James P. Brougham

All Scripture quotations are taken from the
King James Bible.

ISBN# 978-0-6152-0156-6

To order copies, contact the author at:

**James P. Brougham
438 Old Highway 171
Lake Charles, LA 70611**

Published by:

James P. Brougham

Books are available online at:
www.mommysheart.com

Table of Contents

4

Introduction

This book is a result of quality time spent with God in the early hours of the morning over the course of the past several years. These words were given to me in the form of acronyms with a message embodied in each one of them.

As the list grew I was encouraged by my daughter, Kimberly Kane, and members in our prayer group to put the words into book form and share it with others.

Dedication

I want to dedicate this book to…

Sandra Brougham, my wife of 44 years. We've walked a long while together. May the Lord bless us with many more years.

Kimberly, Leslie and Branndon, my children and my heritage.

My four grandchildren: Keaghan, Reigner, Kellyn and Karis. Thank you for allowing me to be called Poppy.

The Tree

In a far away land
On a far away hill
Grew a straight little tree
With a job to fulfill

From a tiny dark seed
Buried deep in the ground
This straight little tree
Sprouted high on a mound

It grew like no other
It grew straighter still
Than all other trees
On that far-away hill

Its leaves were all brighter
Their colors were grand
To all who looked 'bout
In that far-away land

Yet who would have thought
This straight little tree
Would serve such a role
That all 'round would see

Spring turned to Summer
And Winter to Fall
And the straight little tree
Grew from little to tall

It broadened and straightened
With every raindrop that fell
With ever sunbeam that shone
Its story to tell

And as the tree flourished
A Baby was born
Just a small crying tot
That had once a crown worn

No longer a crown
Did He wear on His head
Just some old swaddlin' clothes
And some hay for a bed

And as the Child grew
Something different was there
And his parents soon saw
That their Son was rare

He cared for all others
Before He Himself
He astounded the elders
With His heavenly wealth

Meanwhile on a hill
Grew a straight and tall tree
Its day coming closer
Its job soon to be

The Boy kept on growin'
And soon became Man
Yet never did stray
From His first plan

He taught in the churches
On hillside-in lane
He healed those who dying
Would call out His name

He loved the ones outcast
Thrown out and scorned
He helped the ones helpless
Hearts battered and torn

He soon became known
Throughout that far land
As the Teacher-Messiah
A part of God's hand

Yet some had been placed
On those far-away hills
To turn souls against Him
And conquer their wills

Still He kept on teaching
And preaching the Word
Fulfilling His promise
The voice He had heard

And His Father looked down
And saw His Son's life
He realized His love
To live through such strife

Meanwhile on a hill
Grew a straight and tall tree
Its day coming closer
Its job soon to be

Then finally the day
When both tree and Man
Would finish their jobs
And fulfill the Plan

An angry-scared mob
Would scream "CRUCIFY"
While the silent, strong Teacher
Would give His life-Die

And on that far hill
The tree would be felled
And cut from its trunk
The limbs it once held

Then as the mob frenzied
The Messiah mocked, "King"
A tall, muscled man
To the city the tree bring

The tree fashioned into
A cross – fearful, wide
And placed on a hill
Where many had died

Then up the Place
Of the Skull he is led
And there He and tree
Are finally wed

The flesh of our Savior
Becomes one with the tree
The life of **that Man**
Drains as all there could see

And who would have dreamed
Or dared yet to think
This once scrawny tree
Would be such a link

Yet, in a far away land
On a far-away hill
Grew a straight little tree
Its job – it fulfilled.

Kimberly Page Brougham Kane

BLOOD

Believers
Live
On
Once
Dead

Life for the believer begins when he accepts Christ into his life as his personal Savior. The provision for such an event occurred when Jesus agreed to come to the aid of all mankind. He willingly gave His life's blood for all our sin and bore the stripes on his back for our healing. The blood of Jesus provided man with a new life, which we refer to as eternal or everlasting life. Eternal life with God in heaven is a result of our rebirth. We die out to self so that we can come alive in Christ.

"For as in Adam all die, even so in Christ shall all be made alive" I Corinthians 15:22.

"And so it is written, the first man, Adam, was made a living soul: the last Adam was made a life-giving spirit" I Corinthians 15:45.

"Therefore, if any man be in Christ, he is a new creation: old things are passed away: behold all things are become new" II Corinthians 5:17.

"And you, being dead in your sins and in the uncircumcision of your flesh, hath He made alive together with Him, having forgiven you all trespasses, Blotting out the handwriting of ordinances that was against us, which was contrary to us, and took it out of the way, nailing it to His cross:" Colossians 2:13, 14.

"Verily, verily, I say unto you, He that heareth my word, and believeth on Him that sent me, hath everlasting life, and shall not

come into judgment, but is passed from death unto life" John 5:24.

"And if Christ be in you, the body is dead because of sin, but the Spirit is life because of righteousness" Romans 8:10.

The blood has never and will never lose its power. It continues to do for man that which no other can. It affords everyone the opportunity to plug into eternal life through believing in our heart and confessing with our mouth Jesus as Lord.

BOUND

Being
Overcome
Unquestionably
Needing
Deliverance

We live in a world that is filled with people that are overcome by circumstances and bound up. They are bound by their past, by fear, by bad habits, by alcohol, by drugs, etc. The fact is the provision has been made for their full release and deliverance.

The believer is equipped with faith to operate as an over comer.

"For whatever is born of God overcometh the world; and this is the victory that overcometh the world, even our faith" I John 5:4

God did not say that, as over comers, we would not have tribulation in this life.

"These things I have spoken to you, that in Me ye might have peace. In the world ye shall have tribulation; but be of good cheer; I have overcome the world" John 16:33.

Jesus paid the price for us to be over comers.

"And they overcame him by the blood of the Lamb, and the word of their testimony; and they love not their lives unto the death" Revelations 12:11.

He then handed over the keys to the believer to act with the same power and authority that He enjoyed while living here on earth.

"And I give unto thee the keys to the kingdom of heaven; and whatsoever thou shalt bind on earth shall be bound in heaven;

and whatsoever thou shalt loose on earth shall be loosed in heaven" Matthew 16:19.

You see, Jesus had access to the Father, in whom all power is vested. As believers, we are connected to the Father through the Son, allowing us to operate in the realm of the Father's power.

"For as many as are led by the Spirit of God, they are the sons of God" Romans 8:14.

We become heirs of God's provisions according to His Word. Complete release from the things that bind us up happens when we learn to cast all our care on Him.

"Casting all your care upon Him; for He careth for you" I Peter 5:7.

COVENANT

Contract
One
Views
Everlasting
Never
Adjusted
Not
Temporary

A covenant is an agreement or contract that is binding for all parties named therein. The believer's covenant with God can be viewed as all the promises of God as recorded in the Holy Scriptures. God had no problem reducing to writing His covenant with man. He did so using an unconditional guarantee that He would not change or fail to do exactly as He promised to do in His Word.

"God is not a man that He should lie; neither the son of man that He should repent; hath He said, and shall He not do it? Or hath He spoken, and shall He not make it good" Numbers 23:19.

His covenant with man covers every problem or need that man could experience in a lifetime. It also addresses the requirements we must meet to tap into His unlimited supply of blessings.

"If ye abide in Me and My words abide in you, ye shall ask what ye will, and it shall be done unto you" John 15:7.

"But seek ye first the kingdom of God, and His righteousness: and all these things shall be added unto you" Matthew 6:33.

The Word of God, God's covenant with mankind, is permanent and everlasting.

"Heaven and earth shall pass away, but my words shall not pass away" Matthew 24:35.

"But the word of the Lord endureth for ever. And this is the word which by the gospel is preached unto you" I Peter 1:25.

We are a covenant people serving a covenant God.

CROSS

Christ
Redeemed
Our
Sinful
Soul

Webster defines a cross as an ancient instrument of punishment consisting of an upright stake with a cross piece, to which a person was fastened and left to die. Our redemption is a result of a cross experience; Jesus was nailed to a cross and died for the sin of all mankind.

"And being found in fashion as a man, He humbled Himself and became obedient unto death, even death on the cross" Philippians 2:8.

"Blotting out the handwriting of ordinances that were against us, which was contrary to us, and took it out of the way, nailing it to His cross" Colossians 2:14.

"And having made peace through the blood of His cross, by Him to reconcile all things unto Himself – by Him, I say, whether they be things on earth or things in heaven. And you, that were once alienated and enemies in your mind by wicked works, yet now has He reconciled. In the body of His flesh through death, to present you holy and unblameable and unreprovable in his sight" Colossians 1:20-22.

The Bible instructs us to take up our cross and follow Him. This is the believer's cross experience. This simply means that daily, we need to take on our identity as one of His children and follow Him.

The redemption the believer experiences is a result of Jesus being willing to bare the curse of the law.

"Christ has redeemed us from the curse of the law, being made a curse for us; for it is written, 'Cursed is everyone that hangeth on a tree'" Galatians 3:13.

Jesus paid the debt He did not owe for sin that He did not commit. He willingly took on the sin of all mankind. In doing so, Christ validated our eternal destiny by the shedding of His blood on the cross.

CROWN

Christ
Redefined
Our
Whole
Nature

A crown is often referred to as a symbol of sovereignty. In the case of Jesus, when they placed a crown of thorns on His head, they referred to Him as King of the Jews.

"And when they had plaited a crown of thorns, they put it upon His head, and a reed in His right hand: and they bowed their knee before Him, and mocked Him saying, 'Hail, King of the Jews'" Matthew 27:29.

His obedience to wear a crown of thorns, symbolic of a crown of righteousness, provided man a reward for his new identity. Man would now have a path to the throne of God Almighty through His Son, Jesus Christ.

"For through Him we both have access by one Spirit unto the Father" Ephesians 2:18.

"Henceforth there is laid up for me a crown of righteousness, which the Lord, the righteous judge, shall give me at that day; and not to me only, but unto all them that love His appearing" II Timothy 4:8.

The provision was made and our whole nature was changed from one of sin to one of righteousness.

"For as by one man's disobedience many were made sinners, so by the obedience of one shall many be made righteous" Romans 5:19.

"And if Christ be in you, the body is dead because of sin, but the Spirit is life because of righteousness" Romans 8:10.

The born-again experience that all believers encounter is a result of the Spirit coming alive in them and becoming the dominant force in their lives.

The reward for righteous living is a crown of righteousness for every child of God.

DEATH

Destiny
Encounter
Assured
Through
Humanity

The Christian encounter with death follows a different pattern than that of a non-believer. The Christian dies out to self and turns over the control of the flesh man (Adamic nature) to his heavenly Father through His son, Jesus Christ. This, the first death, takes away the fear of the second death, known as the physical death. The non-believer that lives his entire life controlled by his Adamic nature will experience the physical death never having experienced the new birth.

"And as it is appointed unto men once to die, but after this the judgment" Hebrews 9:27.

This is our destiny encounter which is assured through our human experience. Sin entered the world through Adam and brought with it a close companion known as death.

"Wherefore, as by one man sin entered into the world, and death by sin, and so death passed upon all men, for all have sinned" Romans 5:12.

The believer's reward will be everlasting life according to John 3:16. The non-believer's reward will be an eternity in hell.

"So shall it be at the end of the age: the angels shall come forth, and separate the wicked from among the righteous. And shall cast them into the furnace of fire; there shall be wailing and gnashing of teeth" Matthew 13:49-50.

The path of our destiny is a direct result of a choice we make. We will either accept Christ as Lord and Savior of our lives and will spend an eternity with Him, or we will choose the way of the world and spend an eternity in hell. Choose you this day whom you will serve.

DISCIPLES

Dedicated
Individuals
Serving
Christ
In
Pleasing
Loving
Earthly
Service

A disciple, according to Webster, is one who receives instructions from another, specifically a professed follower. In His earthly ministry, Jesus chose twelve disciples, also referred to as apostles, to serve and assist him. Jesus made it very clear in Luke 14:27 that a true disciple must take up their cross and follow Him.

"And whosoever doth not bear his cross and come after me, cannot be my disciple" Luke 14:27.

A true believer and follower of Christ in discipleship must be willing to go through a period of training according to Acts 11:26.

The natural man does not have the capacity to understand, obey or please God, no matter how gifted or moral he may be. The spirit man like that of the natural man needs instruction and guidance to effectively understand and promote the things of God.

As Christians in the family of God, we need to love without hypocrisy clinging to love and resist that which is evil. We need to be kind and affectionate to one another and fervent in spirit. A true disciple is one that has considered the cost and is willing to pay the price to be a true follower of Christ. Romans 12 is a good outline of the duties and responsibilities of an individual seeking true discipleship.

We are encouraged to live a life that is pleasing to God and are given an example to follow in the life of Enoch.

"And Enoch walked with God, and he was not; for God took him" Genesis 5:24.

We may never reach the level of pleasing God that Enoch did, but we should strive to please Him to the best of our abilities.

DREAM

Desiring
Real
Evidence
Already
Manifested

One of the definitions for dream according to Webster is a "vision of something possible or desirable."

"For God speaketh once, yea twice, yet man perceiveth it not. In a dream, in a vision of the night, when deep sleep falleth upon men, slumberings upon the bed: Then he openeth the ears of men, and sealeth their instructions" Job 33:14-16.

Many times God uses a vision as an avenue to position us to be willing to listen to Him.

A dream can be comforting, instructional, and rewarding with God using angels to deliver His message.

"But while he thought of these things, behold, an angel of the Lord appeared unto him saying, Joseph, thou son of David, fear not take unto thee Mary, thy wife; for that which is conceived in her is of the Holy Spirit" Matthew 1:20.

Joseph, the husband of Mary, found comfort and assurance in his visitation from an angel of the Lord regarding his assignment as the earthly father of Jesus.

Many times a dream can be a warning.

"And being warned of God in a dream that they should not return to Herod, they departed unto their own country another way" Matthew 2:12.

Following God's direction will always result in a path that will lead us away from the snares of evil.

The Word of God is very clear about those that fail to dream.

"Where there is no vision, the people perish; but he that keepeth the law, happy is he" Proverbs 29:18.

Don't be troubled when someone labels you a dreamer.

EASTER

Every
Arrival
Sees
Tomb
Empty
Repeatedly

Mary Magdalene's trip to the tomb the next day after Jesus' crucifixion and burial was one filled with wonder and amazement. She saw the stone that had been used to seal the tomb had been rolled away. She feared someone had taken His body away and ran to tell the disciples of what she had seen and experienced.

She ran into Peter and John along the way and told them of her findings: that the stone had been rolled away, that she feared someone had taken Jesus' body out of the tomb, and that she did not know where they had laid Him. They both ran to the tomb and once there, they went in and found the tomb empty except for Jesus' grave clothes. Once they had determined that the tomb was empty, they went back to their own home.

Mary returned to the tomb weeping. She looked in and saw two angels, one where His head had laid and the other where His feet had laid. The angels spoke to her and questioned her reason for weeping. She responded, "They have taken away my Lord." She turned around and came in contact with Jesus, whom she thought was the gardener. He asked her why she was weeping and she responded by asking Him where He had laid His body. He called her by her name and she recognized Him and called Him Rabboni, which is to say, Master.

She returned to the disciples and advised them that she had spoken to the risen Savior. Her return to the disciples was to confirm that the tomb was empty because he had risen (See John 20). That same story has been told over and over again throughout the ages that the tomb is still empty.

The empty tomb serves to send the message to all generations that this risen Savior is alive and well today.

FAITH

Father's
Assurance
I
Truly
Have

"Now faith is the substance of things hope for, the evidence of things not seen" Hebrews 11:1.

The question could be asked, "How do I get this assurance?" The Word of God says in Romans 10:17, *"So, then faith cometh by hearing, and hearing by the Word of God."*

Many people seem to believe that faith comes literally from hearing the Word of God through our ears. The truth of the matter is that the strength of our faith comes from reading and studying the Word of God.

You see, God speaks to us through His Word when we read it, while we communicate with Him through prayer. The Word we receive when we attend church is simply not enough to sustain us. We must continually be in the Word and listening to God in our spirit for assistance in our daily living.

The Bible also tells us that we cannot please God without faith being present in our lives.

"But without faith it is impossible to please Him; for he that cometh to God must believe that He is, and that He is the rewarder of them that diligently seek Him" Hebrews 11:6.

So then, we see that faith in God comes alive in us at salvation. The Bible says that the measure of faith is given to every believer.

"For I say, through the grace given unto me, to every man that is among you, not to think of himself more highly that he ought to think, but to think soberly, according as God hath dealt to every man the measure of faith" Romans 12:3.

It becomes our responsibility to develop faith beyond our salvation experience. David gave us insight in the Psalms of how to operate using an expanded measure of faith.

"Blessed be the Lord, who daily loadeth us with benefits, even the God of our salvation" Psalms 68:19.

He was simply saying the same faith that was necessary for salvation is all that is necessary for the fullness of God's blessings and benefits.

FAVOR

Father
Always
Values
Our
Relationship

"For thou, Lord, wilt bless the righteous; with favor wilt thou compass him as with a shield" Psalms 5:12.

We quickly learn in our Christian walk that God takes pleasure in blessing the righteous. He also encompasses us with a shield of protection. He then blesses us for separating ourselves from the ungodly and refusing to walk in their counsel.

"Blessed is the man, who walketh not in the counsel of the ungodly, nor standeth in the way of sinners, nor sitteth in the seat of the scornful. But his delight is in the law of the Lord, and in His Law doth he meditate day and night. And he shall be like a tree planted by the rivers of living water; that bringeth forth its fruit in its season; its leaf shall not wither and whatsoever he doeth shall prosper" Psalms 1:1-3.

"Trust in the Lord with all thine heart; and lean not unto thine own understanding. In all thy ways acknowledge him, and he shall direct thy paths" Proverbs 3:5-6.

FORCE

Faith
Once
Released
Crushes
Enemy

Webster describes force as power, violence, or constraint exerted upon a person or thing.

"And from the days of John the Baptist until now the kingdom of heaven suffereth violence, and the violent take it by force" Matthew 11:12.

We have to understand that faith is the force the believer possesses that enables him to deal with the enemy of his soul.

God put a curse on Satan.

"And I will put enmity between thee and the woman, and between thy seed and her seed: it shall bruise thy head, and thou shalt bruise his heel" Genesis 3:15.

Another word for bruise is crush; so when we take our position as a child of God we are operating with the power to crush the head of the enemy.

Faith comes alive when released into the atmosphere through our use of faith-filled words. We have to speak to circumstances and situations and expect to see the desired results. Words out of the mouth a believer are a spiritual force releasing the ability of God within him.

"The prayer of faith shall save the sick, and the Lord shall raise him up; and if he hath committed any sins, they shall be forgiven him" James 5:15.

"If ye abide in me, and my words abide in you, ye shall ask what ye will, and it shall be done unto you" John 15:7.

We position ourselves to receive from God when we allow his Word to abide in us. Every born-again believer operates with a spiritual force within them waiting to be released.

FREE

Full
Release
Enrages
Enemy

"Be sober, be vigilant; because your adversary the devil, as a roaring lion, walketh about, seeking whom he may devour" I Peter 5:8.

It enrages the devil when we are set free from our past through the blood of Jesus.

He is ever-present, trying to trick us into believing that we cannot be set free from our past. We must remind the devil that God made provision for our sins and that He will not remember them.

"I even I, am He who blotteth out thy transgressions for mine our sake, and will not remember thy sins" Isaiah 43:25.

We have an advocate with Father who has made provision for our failures.

"My little children, these things write I unto you, that ye sin not. And if any man sin, we have an advocate with the Father, Jesus Christ the righteous; And He is the propitiation for our sins, and not for our sins only, but also for the sins of the whole world." I John 2:1-2.

We are all seeking full release from our past sins. We fail to realize that God will not hear our cry in time of need if we harbor sin in our heart representing things from our past.

"If I regard iniquity in my heart, the Lord will not hear me" Psalms 66:18.

We cannot be tricked by the devil into believing that if no one other than God knows about it, we are OK.

The devil is still mad because he was cast out of heaven by God.

"And he said unto them, I beheld Satan as lightening fall from heaven" Luke 10:18.

Christ gave unto the believer power to deal with the enemy of our soul that was cast out of heaven.

"Behold, I give unto you power to tread on serpents and scorpions, and over the power of the enemy; and nothing shall by any means hurt you" Luke 10:19.

We walk in freedom, for the word of God says that whom the Son has set free is free indeed. We are free to enjoy the fullness of God's blessings and live overcoming lives. We can truly say that Christ in me is the hope of glory. Christ in us allows us to be in the very presence of God and under the umbrella of His protection and grace.

GIFTS

God's
Investment
Features
True
Service

"For the gifts and calling of God are without repentance"
Romans 11:29.

Once we have experienced Salvation and are brought into the family of God as one of His children, we must now take on our responsibility as a member of the family.

"Then said Jesus to His disciples, if any man will come after me, let him deny himself, and take up his cross, and follow me"
Matthew16:24.

It is important for us to recognize that Adam's disobedience to God's instructions made it necessary for God to unveil the complete plan He had for mankind.

His plan included the gift of His son, the Lord Jesus Christ. By giving His son as the supreme sacrifice, God ushered in the dispensation of Grace.

God does not call us to do something that He will not properly equip us to do. He equips us with spiritual gifts that will be necessary for our success and service. The church of Jesus Christ functions as a representative of God in a lost and dying world.

Our journey with God begins with our first and most important gift of all, eternal life.

"For the wages of sin is death, but the Gift of God is Eternal Life through Jesus Christ our Lord" Romans 6:23.

Once we have accepted the gift of eternal life, we are now positioned to receive other gifts that God has available for us.

The church of today cannot effectively minister to the total needs of mankind without the gifts outlined in I Corinthians 12:8-10 being present and in operation. We cannot expect God to pour out His blessings upon us if we never move beyond salvation in our Christian experience. We remain as babes in Christ without ever experiencing the fullness of His blessings.

The gifts all have a common thread, that of faith.

"For by grace are you saved through faith; that not of yourselves: it is the gift of God" Ephesians 2:8.

This faith in a living God enables us to live in an earthly body in a heavenly manner. We are equipped to house the gifts of the Spirit within us as children of a Holy God.

GIVING

God's
Interest
Validated
In
New
Growth

The Word of God is very clear about giving, and the manner in which we are to give. When we learn to give God His share of everything we have, we can get ready for God to open the windows of heaven for us.

"Bring all the tithes unto the storehouse, that there may be food in mine house, and test me now herewith, saith the Lord of hosts, if I will not open for you the windows of heaven, and pour out for you a blessing, that there shall not be room enough to receive it" Malachi 3:10.

"But this I say, He who soweth sparingly shall also reap sparingly; and he that soweth bountifully shall reap also bountifully. Every man according as he purposeth in his heart, so let him give, not grudgingly, or of necessity; for God loveth a cheerful giver." II Corinthians 9:6-7.

The key that opens the door of receiving is giving.

"Give and it shall be given unto you; good measure pressed down, and shaken together, and running over, shall men give into your bosom. For with the same measure that ye measure it shall be measured to you again" Luke 6:38.

When we freely give we can also expect to freely receive.

"....freely ye have received, freely give" Matthew 10:8.

A loving relationship with the Father through His Son, Jesus Christ, positions the believer to receive God's best.

"Beloved, I wish above all things that thou mayeth prosper and be in good health, even as thy soul prospereth" III John 2.

"That I may cause those who love me to inherit substance; and I will fill their treasuries" Proverbs 8:21.

GLAD

Glorified
Living
Always
Delivers

"If ye abide in me, and my words abide in you, ye shall ask what ye will, and it shall be done unto you. In this is my Father glorified, that ye bear much fruit; so shall ye be my disciples" **John 15:7-8.**

The Word of God is very clear about His desire to bless us in abundance when we learn to abide in Him and allow His Word to abide in us. When we ask of the Father we should expect to receive from Him.

"Verily, verily, I say unto you, He that believeth on me, the works that I do shall he do also; and greater works than these shall ye do, because I go unto my Father. And whatever ye shall ask in my name, that will I do, that the Father may be glorified in the Son. If ye shall ask anything in my name, I will do it" **John 14:12-14.**

A true relationship with the Father through his Son, Jesus Christ, positions every believer to be in line to receive God's very best.

We see our advocate, Jesus Christ, in action in the 18th chapter of John's gospel. He was quick to present His close followers to His Father, seeking approval for a relationship with them like He and the Father enjoyed. The relationship referred to here was oneness in spirit.

Our reward for being followers of His Son is one of having access to the Father.

"I pray for them; I pray not for the world, but for them whom thou hast given me; for they are thine. And all mine are thine; and I am glorified in them. And now I am no more in the world, but these are in the world, and I come to thee Holy Father, keep through thine own name those whom thou has given me, that they may be one, as we are" John 17:9-11.

"Moreover, whom he did predestinate, them he also called; and whom he called, them he also justified, them he also glorified. What shall we then say to these things? If God be for us, who can be against us? He that spared not his own Son, but delivered him up for us all, how shall he not with him also freely give us all things" Romans 8:30-32.

God desires a close relationship with His followers and that relationship brings with it His hedge of protection. He is quick to point out that if He is for us, the devil and all his forces are no match for Him.

GLORY

God's
Love
Overflows
Reaching
You

The Greek word for glory is *doxa*. God's glory is the visible manifestation of God's nature, ability and character. We are the sum total of our nature, ability and character.

The love of God for man was expressed in the greatest manner possible.

"For God so loved the world that He gave His only begotten Son, that whosoever believeth in Him should not perish, but have everlasting life" John 3:16.

"Greater love hath no man than this, that a man lay down his life for his friends" John 15:13.

We see this love overflowing from God and filling the earth with His glory.

"But as truly as I live, all the earth shall be filled with the glory of the Lord" Numbers 14:21.

"And blessed be His glorious name forever; and let the whole earth be filled with His glory. Amen, and Amen" Psalms 72:19.

"And one cried unto another, and said holy, holy, holy is the Lord of hosts; the whole earth is full of His glory" Isaiah 6:3.

God's glory serves to change each of us into His image.

"But we all with unveiled face beholding as in a mirror the glory of the Lord, are changed into the same image from glory to glory, even as by the Spirit of the Lord" II Corinthians 3:18.

Every believer is given the opportunity to benefit from the glory of God through our relationship with Him through His Son, Jesus Christ.

GOD

Greatest
Only
Deity

"The eternal God is the refuge, and underneath are the everlasting arms; and he shall thrust out the enemy from before thee, and shall say, destroy them" Deuteronomy 33-27.

God provides His children with a safety net represented by His everlasting arms that are always there to hold us up.

In the Psalms, David expressed the support of God coming in the form of Him upholding us with His hand. When we learn to acknowledge Him as Lord and master of our lives, then all the benefits of being a part of the family of God are at our disposal.

"The steps of a good man are ordered by the Lord, and He delighted in his way. Though he fall, he shall not be utterly cast down; for the Lord upholdeth him with His hand" Psalms 37:23-24.

"O Lord of hosts, God of Israel, who dwelleth between the cherubim, thou art the God, even thou alone, of all the kingdoms of the earth; thou hath made heaven and earth" Isaiah 37:16.

"Thus saith the Lord, the King of Israel, and his redeemer, the Lord of hosts; I am the first, and I am the last, and besides me there is no God" Isaiah 44:6.

"Look unto me, and be saved, all the ends of the earth; for I am God, and there is none else" Isaiah 45:22.

"And the scribe said unto him, Well, Master, thou hath said the truth; for there is one God, and there is no other but he" Mark 12:32.

God is very clear about His position as the one and only God. He is a jealous God and will not accept anything but the number one position in our lives.

GRACE

God
Redeemed
Adam
Condemnation
Eternally

Grace, as defined by Webster, is divine mercy or forgiveness. God's love for man was expressed in a supernatural way when He paid a ransom to deliver and redeem man from the bondage of sin. He gave his only Son, Jesus Christ, so that man could be set free.

"Who gave himself for us, that He might redeem us from all iniquity, and purify unto himself a peculiar people, of His own, zealous of good works" Titus 2:14.

"But not as the offense, so also is the free gift. For if through the offense of one many be dead, much more the grace of God, and the gift of grace, which is by one man, Jesus Christ hath abounded unto many" Romans 5:15.

It was through Adam's sin that the sentence of death was pronounced upon all mankind.

"Wherefore, as by one man sin entered into the world, and death by sin; and so death passed upon all men, for that all have sinned" Romans 5:12.

We will all experience a destiny encounter that is assured through humanity.

We were all condemned as a result of the judgment that came upon man because of Adam's sin.

"Therefore as by the offense of one judgment came upon all men to condemnation; even so by the righteousness of one the free gift came upon all men unto justification of life" Romans 5:18.

Through the grace of God every believer is made eternally secure. God gave His best so that we could have access to His best through His son, Jesus Christ.

In the following scripture, we see Jesus in action as our intercessor as children of grace.

"These words spake Jesus, and lifted up his eyes to heaven, and said, Father, the hour is come to glorify thy Son, that the Son may also glorify thee: As though hast given him power over all flesh, that he should give eternal life to as many as though hast given him. And this is life eternal, that they might know thee the only true God, and Jesus Christ whom thou hath sent" John 17:1-3.

GUILT

Greatest
Underlying
Indicator
Limiting
Triumph

Virtually everyone living carries around with them a measure of guilt for something they have done or not done in the course of their life. It is easy to identify but not so easy to deal with. We allow the devil to make us believe that our past shortcomings will limit our future triumphs.

Many times, the guilt of our past is a factor that, if allowed, will limit future successes in our lives. We must quickly identify the root cause of our guilt being the sin of omission or the sin of commission and take the necessary action to correct it.

"If we confess our sins, He is faithful and just, to forgive our sins, and to cleanse us from all unrighteous" I John 1:9.

Guilt brings with it a close companion called doubt. Doubt, if allowed to remain, permits guilt to get a stronghold on our life. Because of the close connection between guilt and doubt, we must break the stronghold of doubt so that we can adequately deal with guilt. We must come to the realization that the antidote for doubt is faith.

"For verily I say unto you, that whosoever shall say unto this mountain, Be thou removed, and be thou cast into the sea; and shall not doubt in his heart, but believe that those things he saith shall come to pass; he shall have whatsoever he saith" Mark 11:23.

Once doubt is adequately dealt with, then guilt can be displaced with faith. Faith teaches us to disregard those thoughts of guilt because thoughts that are not put into words or actions die unborn.

"He that keepeth his mouth keepeth his life; but he that openeth his lips shall have destruction" Proverbs 13:3.

When we learn to control our thoughts then God can prove Himself to us.

"For as he thinketh in his heart, so is he; eat and drink saith he to thee; but his heart is not with thee" Proverbs 23:7.

HEALING

His
Ever
Abiding
Love
Imparts
Needed
Gift

According to Webster, healing is the process of curing or restoring an individual to a sound or healthy condition. God addressed the provision for healing in the Old Testament in the Book of Isaiah.

When man sinned against God, divine health was taken away and sickness was an issue that every man would have to deal with until the Son of God came on the scene.

"But He was wounded for our transgressions, He was bruised for our iniquities: the chastisement of our peace was upon Him, and with His stripes we are healed" Isaiah 53:5.

The issue of sickness addressed in the New Testament was not a prophetic statement as seen in Isaiah 53:5 but rather a provision or remedy for all our sicknesses and diseases.

"Who His own self bore our sins in His own body, on the tree, that we, being dead to sins, should live unto righteousness: by whose stripes ye were healed" I Peter 2:24.

This is all a result of a love between God and His creation, mankind. God describes His love for man in John 3:16

"For God so loved the world, that He gave His only begotten Son, that whosoever believeth in Him should not perish, but have everlasting life."

The price has been paid and the provision made for all manors of sickness and disease that man may encounter while living here on earth. We deal with all sickness and disease in the past tense because the Word of God clearly states by whose stripes ye were healed. It is just a matter of accepting what is already ours. We serve a great big loving God.

JOY

Jesus
Overshadows
You

Joy could be defined as an outward expression of an inner feeling.

"...for the joy of the Lord is your strength" Nehemiah 8:10.

We draw from His strength by being in His presence.

"Thou wilt show me the path of life. In thy presence is the fullness of joy, at thy right hand there are pleasures for evermore" Psalms 16:11.

We see in I Peter 1:8 that it is very hard to describe the joy experienced by the believer.

"Whom, having not seen, ye love; in whom, though now ye see Him not, yet believing, ye rejoice with joy unspeakable and full of glory" I Peter 1:8.

Joy comes from a face to face encounter with Jesus.

"Having many things to write unto you, I would not write with paper and ink, but I trust to come unto you, and speak face to face, that your joy may be full" II John 1:12.

The joy of Lord is but a shadow of things to come.

"Now unto Him that is able to keep you from falling, and to present you faultless before the presence of his glory with exceeding joy" Jude 24.

The overshadowing joy of Jesus is a secret place of security.

"He who dwelleth in the secret place of the Most High shall abide under the shadow of the Almighty" Psalms 91:1.

A shadow as described by Webster is an inseparable companion. The joy of the Lord is an inseparable companion that allows us to be in the very presence of the Rock of Ages.

"He is the Rock, His work is perfect; for all His ways are justice; a God of truth and without iniquity, just and right is He" Deuteronomy 32:4.

In the shadow of the Almighty we enjoy protection, comfort and provision.

"And a man shall be like an hiding place from the wind, and a covert from the tempest; like rivers of water in a dry place, like the shadow of a great rock in weary land" Isaiah 32:2.

JUDGE

Jesus
Understands
Divine
Godly
Examination

Webster defines a judge as one who is a qualified evaluator. This clearly identifies Jesus Christ as one qualified to be a judge for all mankind.

"For we have not a high priest who cannot be touched with the feeling of our infirmities, but was in all points tempted like as we are, yet without sin" Hebrews 4:15.

Christ had no character flaws, making him the most qualified individual to serve in the capacity of Supreme Judge.

"Jesus Christ the same yesterday, and today and forever" Hebrews 13:8.

Christ came into the world as a Savior for all mankind, and then willingly gave His life for our sins so that we could be reunited with the Father. He then took on the identity of mediator for man until such time as He will assume His identity as the Supreme Judge of all mankind.

"For there is on God, and one mediator between God and men, the man, Jesus Christ" I Timothy 2:5.

"For the Father judgeth no man, but hath committed all judgment unto the Son" John 5:22.

It is very clear that Jesus will soon take on His assignment as Supreme Judge. Man will not have the opportunity to ask for a jury trial based on evidence presented but will rather have to face the Supreme Judge with an open book containing all the evidence. It is very important to note that each of us determines where we will spend eternity.

JUDGMENT

Justly
Unveiling
Deeds
Governing
Man's
Eternity
Now
Told

Judgment, says Webster, is the pronouncing of a formal opinion or decision; also, the opinion or decision given.

"But after thy hardness and impenitent heart treasurest up unto thyself wrath against the day of wrath and revelation of the righteous judgment of God; who will render to every man according to his deeds" Romans 2:5-6.

We will not be able to hide or withhold anything from the Son of God on the Day of Judgment; all our hidden secrets will be revealed. Every deed will be exposed.

"To them who by patient continuance in well doing seek for glory and honour and immortality, eternal life. But unto them that are contentious, and do not obey the truth, but obey unrighteousness, indignation and wrath" Romans 2:7-8.

"But the Lord shall endure for ever; he hath prepared his throne for judgment. And he shall judge the world in righteousness; he shall minister judgment to people in uprightness" Psalms 9:7-8.

We are all going to have to experience the judgment of the Son of God.

"And as it is appointed unto men once to die, but after this the judgment" Hebrews 9:27.

Judgment is going to be harsh on the unbeliever and nations that forget God.

"The wicked shall be turned into hell, and all the nations that forget God" Psalms 9:17.

God will not be the judge in the Day of Judgment because He has committed all judgment unto His Son.

"For the Father judgeth no man, but hath committed all judgment unto his Son" John 5:22.

When all man's deeds are unveiled then his eternity will be pronounced by the Supreme Judge, the Son of God.

KNOW

Knowledge
Needs
Overshadowing
Wisdom

According to Webster, to know is to be fully informed. To know simply means we have spent the time to become knowledgeable in a given area or about a specific thing through study and observation. Wisdom is the ability to properly apply and use knowledge.

"That the God of our Lord Jesus Christ, the Father of glory may give unto you the spirit of wisdom and revelation in the knowledge of Him" Ephesians 1:17.

We can readily see that the knowledge of God coupled with the indwelling of His Spirit allows us to operate in His revelation knowledge arena. The natural man cannot know the things of God because the Spirit of God is not present to reveal them to him. The spirit of God's wisdom coupled with the knowledge of God serves to lead us into all truths.

We as children of God need to study and apply His word to our lives on a daily basis so that we walk in a manner that pleases our Heavenly Father.

"Study to show thyself approved unto God, a workman that needeth not to be ashamed, rightly dividing the word of truth" II Timothy 2:15.

"The heart of the wise teachest his mouth, and addeth learning to his lips" Proverbs 16:23.

The spirit of one possessing wisdom controls what comes out of his mouth, thus allowing God to speak through him with words that will confound even the wise.

LEGACY

Living
Example
Gave
All
Changing
You

Legacy, according to Webster, is something that is left to future generations. The greatest legacy ever was what Jesus did for each of us. His death, burial and resurrection provided mankind with a solution to the sin problem in his life. The blood of Jesus ushered in the dispensation of grace and gave back to man what Adam had taken away: the ability to be in the very presence of God.

What better legacy could we leave to those who come after us than to have them say; he was truly a child of the living God?

"Let no man despise thy youth; but be thou an example of the believers, in word, in conversation, in charity, in spirit, in faith, in purity" I Timothy 4:12.

Our instructions are very clear as to how we are live our daily lives and the steps we should take.

"For even hereunto were ye called; because Christ also suffered for us, leaving us an example, that ye follow His steps" I Peter 2:21.

God is the God of the living and not the God of the dead.

"I am the God of Abraham, and the God of Isaac, and the God of Jacob? God is not the God of the dead, but of the living" Matthew 22:32.

"I am the living bread which came down from heaven: if any man eat of the bread he shall live for ever: and the bread that I will give is my flesh, which I will give for the life of the world" *John 6:51.*

We are changed forever more through our relationship with Jesus.

"Verily, verily, I say unto you, he that heareth my word, and believeth on Him that sent me, hath everlasting life, and shall not come into condemnation, but is passed from death unto life" *John 5:24.*

LIGHT

Logged
Into
God's
Hidden
Treasure

"But if we walk in the Light, as He is the Light, we have fellowship one with another, and the blood of Jesus Christ, His Son, cleanses us from all sin" I John 1:7.

If we log into God's hidden treasure of fellowship, recognizing that believers live on once dead to self (Salvation), we allow God to change and control our Satan-inspired nature through Jesus Christ His Son.

"For ye were once darkness, but now are ye light in the Lord: walk as children of light" Ephesians 5:8.

For you were without Christ and walking in darkness, but now you are logged into God's hidden treasure through His Son, the Lord Jesus Christ, and now walk as children of light.

We log into the hidden treasures of God when we learn to spend time alone with Him.

"If ye abide in me, and my words abide in you, ye shall ask what you will, and it shall be done unto you" John 15:7.

"Delight thyself in the Lord, and He shall give thee the desires of thine heart" Psalms 37:4

We position ourselves to receive the very desires of our heart when we take delight in serving the Lord.

When we learn to walk in the proper manner before God He will bless beyond measure.

"For the Lord God is a sun and shield; the Lord will give grace and glory. No good thing will he withhold from them that walk uprightly" Psalms 84:11.

Godly living brings God on the scene to walk with us through every trial we may face in life's journey. God's presence brings strength to our weakness and light to our darkness.

LOVE

Lowest
One
Valued
Equal

"For God so loved the world, that He gave His only begotten Son, that whosoever believeth in Him should not perish, but have everlasting life" John 3:16.

Please note the word whosoever; it means exactly what it says. God does not put requirements on His selection for those who will be given everlasting life according to race, gender, education, age, achievements, or social status. Every person is valued equal in the eyes of God. We all begin our journey with Jesus on a level playing field.

God is in search of those whose heart is right and not the position that they may currently hold.

"...for the Lord seeth not as man seeth; for man looketh on the outward appearance, but the Lord looketh on the heart" I Samuel 16:7.

God's love is an everlasting love that will not change.

"The Lord hath appeared of old unto me, saying, Yea, I have loved thee with an everlasting love: therefore with loving kindness have I drawn thee" Jeremiah 31:3.

We are all valued equal in the eyes of God, and His desire is to bring us into His family as one of His children through salvation, so that He can bless us with abundance.

"Blessed be the Lord, who daily loaded us with benefits, even the God of our Salvation" Psalms 68:19.

We must recognize that the same faith that we use for salvation is the same faith that we must use for every other need we may have spiritually, financially, physically or emotionally.

MERCY

Making
Everything
Right
Concerning
You

The definition of mercy is described by Webster as, "the disposition to forgive, spare or pity; compassion; an act of clemency; compassionate treatment." God's mercy can readily be seen in the way He handled His disappointment of man's sin. God didn't turn His back on man and walk away from him as we may have. He rather unveiled His master plan for all mankind that involved both mercy and grace.

"So then, it is not of him that willeth, nor of him that runneth, but of God that showeth mercy" Romans 9:16.

No one but God could administer His sovereign will in extending His mercy to all mankind. His master plan included a provision for man to be reunited with Him through a special gift in the form of His son, Jesus Christ. We can readily say that mercy rewrote our lives.

We must be ready to present our bodies a living sacrifice unto God when mercy comes on the scene to give new direction to our lives.

"I beseech you therefore, brethren, by the mercies of God, that ye present your bodies a living sacrifice, holy acceptable unto God, which is your reasonable service" Romans 12:1.

When Jesus came on the scene as the Son of God, He brought with Him the key to every need man had, including eternal life. Through our relationship with the Father through His son, Jesus Christ, we are the recipients of God's mercy.

God gave his very best so that we would be positioned to be able to receive the best He has for each of us.

"Blessed be the God and the Father of our Lord Jesus Christ, who, according to His abundant mercy, hath begotten us again unto a living hope by the resurrection of Jesus Christ from the dead. To an inheritance incorruptible, and undefiled, and that fadeth not away, reserved in heaven for you" *I Peter 1:3-4.*

MIND

Man's
Intellect
Needs
Direction

The Bible has a great deal to say about the mind. Here are just a few examples.

"Trust in the Lord with all thine heart; and lean not to thine own understanding (mind)" Proverbs 3:5.

"Casting down imaginations (reasoning), and every high thing that exalteth itself against the knowledge of God, and bringing into captivity every thought (thinking) to the obedience of Christ" II Corinthians 10:5.

"And be not conformed to this world; but be ye transformed by the renewing of your mind, that ye may prove what is that good and acceptable, and perfect will of God" Romans 12:2

The renewing of the mind occurs when we study and apply the Word of God to our lives. Scripture in I Corinthians 2:16 teaches us to have the mind of Christ. The Adam nature cannot know the things of God without the occurrence of a renewed mind. That is, a transformation must occur and the old Adam nature that is wrapped in carnality must succumb to being controlled led by the Spirit of God.

The mind, once it comes under the control of the Holy Spirit, causes our reasoning and thinking to focus on God as the supplier of our every need. God is truly the author and finisher of our faith. A mind focused on God is easily led into all truths. God opens His door of understanding and blessings when we allow our minds to be controlled and directed by the Holy Spirit.

The only way the natural man can realize the fullness of God's blessings is to allow the spirit man to control his life. Because of the spirit man's relationship with God, God makes him an heir to every thing that God has. We must understand that we are named in the Father's will and that every good and perfect thing is available to us as children of a Holy God.

MONEY

Materialism's
Overwhelming
Nature
Entraps
You

The world gauges the success or failure of an individual by his material possessions. This opens the door for materialism's influence to distort our vision and thinking and cause us to put a high priority on material possessions. This allows the love of money and what it can bring, to become a god to us. At this point we have tapped into the root cause of all evil, the love of money.

"For the love of money is the root of all evil, which while some coveted after, they have erred from the faith, and pierced themselves through with many sorrows" I Timothy 6:10.

God will not take a back seat to any other god.

"No man can serve two masters; for either he will hate the one, and love the other; or else he will hold to the one, and despise the other. Ye cannot serve God and money" Matthew 6:24.

The love of money separates us from the love of God when it becomes our god. This separation is like a cancer that just keeps eating away until it completely controls and destroys you. We are ultimately consumed with greed, which cannot be satisfied with any amount of money or the things it can buy. The spirit man cannot be satisfied with material things. The irony of it all is that the natural man cannot be satisfied with the material things either.

MORALS

Master
Ordained
Rules
Alters
Lives
Significantly

Morals could be described as dealing or concerned with establishing principles of right and wrong in behavior. It is the single most important element affecting society today. When we lose our ability to distinguish between right and wrong we are destined for failure and defeat.

The Word of God in very clear about how unrighteousness or wrong is treated.

"Know ye not that the unrighteous shall not inherit the kingdom of God! Be not deceived; neither fornicators, nor idolaters, nor adulterers, nor effeminate, nor abusers of themselves with mankind, nor thieves, nor covetous, nor drunkards, nor revilers, nor extortioners, shall inherit the kingdom of God" I Corinthians 6:9-10.

God gives us a clear path to follow in dealing with our Adamic nature.

"Finally brethren, whatever things are true, whatever things are honest, whatever things are just, whatever things are pure, whatever things are lovely, whatever things are of good report; if there be any virtue, and if there be any praise think on these things" Philippians 4:8.

When we choose to follow Christ in building our Christian character our lives will be dominated and controlled by the fruit of the Spirit.

"But the fruit of the spirit is love, joy, peace, lone suffering, gentleness, goodness, faith, meekness, self-control; against such there is no law" Galatians 5:22-23.

OBEY

Once
Believing
Ever
Yielding

"And Samuel said, Hath the Lord as great delight in burnt offerings and sacrifices, as in obeying the voice of the Lord? Behold to obey is better than sacrifice, and to hearken that the fat of rams" I Samuel 15:22.

We can only realize the full potential of our Christian walk when we learn to trust and obey God.

"And the people said unto Joshua, The Lord our God will we serve, and His voice will we obey" Joshua 24:24.

The word teaches us that obedience is better than sacrifice.

As we study the Word of God we can understand why this statement is so important. Obedience as portrayed by Mary, the mother of Jesus, was an act that changed the course of all mankind. Her obedience opened the door for God to unveil His master plan of redemption. Her willful obedience mastered the old Adam nature and dealt sin a death-defying blow through the blood of Jesus at Calvary.

The willingness of Jesus Christ to come into the world as the supreme sacrifice gives every believer the opportunity to have access to the Father. Jesus, through an act of obedience, fulfilled His role as redeemer through His birth, death, and resurrection. He now sits at the right hand of God ever making intercession for each of us.

PAST

Pursuing
After
Spent
Time

Christians should always question flash backs from their past. This is a ploy the devil uses to confuse us and make us believe that our past equals our future. The fact is God provided a way out for us. God not only forgives us of our past but also forgets about it as well.

"And their sins and iniquities will I remember no more" Hebrews 10:17.

"I, even I, am He who blotteth out thy transgressions for mine own sake, and will not remember thy sins" Isaiah 43:25.

Anytime we find ourselves drifting back to the past in our thinking, we should immediately question the source of these thoughts. We are reminded by God through His Word in John 10:10 that the thief cometh but to steal, kill and destroy. He comes to steal our victory, kill our faith and destroy our relationship with God.

We spend a lot of our time reflecting back on things that occurred in our past. These experiences may become stumbling blocks, preventing us from making changes that will positively affect our future. If we have changed the way we conduct our lives, the past should serve as a teacher of lessons learned and not as an indicator of things to come.

"Whom God hath set forth to be a propitiation through faith in His blood, to declare His righteousness for the remission of sins that are past, through the forbearance of God" Romans 3:25.

We must agree to change and put off the former manner of life and forget about the past.

"That ye put off concerning the former manner of life the old man, which is corrupt according to the deceitful lusts, and be renewed in the spirit of your mind. And that ye put on the new man, which after God is created in righteousness and true holiness" Ephesians 4:22-24.

Remember the devil can only remind you about your past and that God alone knows your future.

"For God so loved the world, that He gave His only begotten Son, that whosoever believeth in Him should not perish, but have everlasting life" John 3:16.

"For the Lord God is a sun and shield; the Lord will give grace and glory. No good thing will He withhold from them that walks uprightly" Psalm 84:11.

Don't allow the devil to control your future by listening to his lies about your past.

POWER

Possessing
One
Whom
Enemy
Respects

"But ye shall receive power after that the Holy Spirit is come upon you and you shall be witnesses unto me both in Jerusalem, and in all Judea, and in Samaria, and to the uttermost part of the earth" Acts 1:8.

"But if you shall indeed obey His voice and do all that I speak, then will I be an enemy unto your enemies, and an adversary unto your adversaries" Exodus 23:22.

The best example of the power possessed by a child of God was given to us when Jesus was confronted by the devil after returning from the Jordan. He was being led by the Spirit into the wilderness. He was quick to remind the devil who His father was and the power He possessed as a representative of a Holy God.

"And Jesus answered, and said unto him, get thee behind me, Satan; for it is written, thou shalt worship the Lord, thy God, and Him only shalt thou serve" Luke 4:8.

Jesus found it important to document in writing what His intentions were for His followers. We would possess the same Holy Spirit that was available to Him in His earthly tenure. We could follow His example when confronted by the devil by pointing the devil to the written Word of God. The Word of God has never lost any of its power and is readily available to every child of God.

In John 14, we find Jesus' promise to believers that we can step into His shoes and do the works that He did. We can be about the

Father's business acting in His full authority as members of the family of God.

"Verily, verily, I say unto you, he that believeth on me, the works that I do shall he do also; and greater works that these shall he do, because I go unto the Father. And whatever ye shall ask in my name, that will I do, that the Father may be glorified in the Son. If ye shall ask anything in my name, I will do it" John 14:12-14.

We possess overcoming power as members of the family of God. In the book of Revelation, we find we possess overcoming power that the enemy of our soul has to respect.

"And they overcame him by the Blood of the Lamb, and by the word of their testimony; and they loved not their lives unto the death" Revelations 12:11.

PRIDE

Purposely
Refusing
Instruction
Determined
Essential

Pride can be helpful or destructive. We can see pride that is helpful in action when we see a person taking pride in doing a good job. From this comes the expression, he takes pride in what he does. His motive is right because his endeavor is not only to please himself, but someone else.

Pride can be very destructive when a person allows it to take over and distort the way he thinks and conducts his life. We simply refuse to make the necessary changes to our lives that God requires of us to be effective as workers in His Kingdom.

"Let not the foot of pride come against me, and let not the hand of the wicked remove me" Psalms 36:11.

"Therefore, pride compasseth them about like a chain; violence covereth them like a garment" Psalms 73:6.

"Pride goeth before destruction, and a haughty spirit before a fall" Proverbs 16:18.

We need to avoid pride and not allow it to have a place in our heart. The Word of God teaches us to hate pride and to be careful how we speak.

"The fear of the Lord is to hate evil; pride and arrogance, and the evil way, and the perverse mouth, do I hate" Proverbs 8:13.

"In the mouth of the foolish is a rod of pride, but the lips of the wise shall preserve them" Proverbs 14:3.

We must recognize that those things that enter into the mouth of man defileth not a man, but rather those things that come out of his mouth. Pride is one of those things that comes out of the mouth of man from within.

"Not that which goeth in the mouth defileth a man, but that which cometh out of the mouth, this defileth a man" Matthew 15:11.

We cannot allow pride to separate us from the love of God by refusing to abide by the instructions outlined in His Word.

PROMISE

Prophesied
Restoration
Of
Man's
Inward
Spirit
Ensured

A promise gives ground for hope and expectation. It is very important for the believer to understand that whenever God makes a promise, He can perform.

"And being fully persuaded that what He had promised, He was able also to perform" Romans 4:21.

"Let us hold fast the profession of our faith without wavering (for He is faithful that promised)" Hebrews 10:23.

In Isaiah 59:20-21 we see the coming of Jesus prophesied.

"And the Redeemer shall come to Zion, and unto those who turn from transgression in Jacob, saith the Lord. And for me, this is my covenant with them, saith the Lord: My Spirit that is upon thee."

He has restored and sealed us with the earnest of the Spirit.

"Who hath sealed us, and given the earnest of the Spirit in our hearts" II Corinthians 1:22.

Sin separated man from God and the precious blood of Jesus redeemed us. God's love for man was so strong that He gave His only Son for the cause of man.

"For God so loved the world, that He gave His only begotten Son, that whosoever believeth in Him should not perish, but have everlasting life." John 3:16.

The indwelling of His Spirit gives the believer access to the throne room of God Almighty. In the book of Zechariah, we see that the things that will be accomplished for God that will count will be done through His Spirit.

"Then he answered and spoke unto me saying, this is the word of the Lord to Zerubbabel, saying, Not by might, not by power, but by my Spirit, sayeth the Lord of hosts" Zechariah 4:6.

In the Psalms, David makes us aware of the need for repositioning ourselves for God's restoration process.

"Restore unto me the joy of thy salvation, and uphold me with a willing spirit" Psalms 51:12.

The repositioning process is necessary because all we like sheep have gone astray according to Isaiah 53:6.

It is important for every believer to know that each promise God makes comes with an unconditional warranty.

"For all the promises of God in Him are yea, and in Him Amen, unto the glory of God by us" II Corinthians 1:20.

REDEMPTION

Redefining
Eternal
Destiny
Erasing
Man's
Past
Tragedy
Involving
Ones
Nature

Redemption is a process whereby man's past sin nature comes in contact with the Blood of Jesus and is immediately transformed into a Christ-like nature.

"In whom we have redemption through His blood, the forgiveness of sins, according to the riches of His grace" Ephesians 1:7.

"For ye are bought with a price; therefore, glorify God in your body and in your spirit, which are God's" I Corinthians 6:20.

When we become the redeemed of Jesus Christ, our past does not dictate or equal our future.

"Christ has redeemed us from the curse of the law, being made a curse for us; for it is written, Cursed is everyone that hangeth on a tree; That the blessings of Abraham might come on the Gentiles through Jesus Christ, that we might receive the promise of the Spirit through faith" Galatians 3:13-14.

"Therefore if any man be in Christ, he is a new creation; old things are passed away; behold, all things are become new" II Corinthians 5:17.

The tragedy that man faced when Adam disobeyed God and sinned was erased by the obedience of the second Adam to walk in perfection before His Father.

"And so it is written, the first man, Adam, was made a living soul; the last Adam was made a quickening spirit" I Corinthians 15:45.

We actually become partakers of the divine nature of God as believers.

"By which are given unto us exceedingly great and precious promises, that by these we might be partakers of the divine nature, having escaped the corruption that is in the world through lust" II Peter 1:4.

REPENT

Regret
Evil
Past
Embracing
Needed
Truth

Repentance is the only way we can renew our relationship with God once we have sinned. We have to regret our evil past, turn away from our sin, and willingly follow God's plan for our lives.

"If they fall away, to renew them again unto repentance, seeing they crucify to themselves the Son of God afresh, and put Him to an open shame" Hebrews 6:6.

Truth is the only way to restore a broken relationship with God.

"Jesus saith unto him, I am the way, the truth, and the life; no man cometh unto the Father, but by me" John 14:6.

Truth and the Word are adjectives describing the nature of Jesus. When we recognize that the Word is our source of power and strength, we position ourselves to live an overcoming life.

"In the beginning was the Word, and the Word was with God, and the Word was God" John 1:1.

The Word has to become a lamp unto our feet and a light unto our path so that when we get sidetracked, we can find our way back to God.

"Thy word is a lamp unto my feet and a light unto my path" Psalms 119:105.

To be set free from our evil past we must desire the truth.

"And ye shall know the truth, and the truth shall make you free"
John 8:32.

We must allow truth to be our guide.

"Nevertheless, when He, the Spirit of truth, is come, He will
guide you into all truth; He shall not speak of Himself , but
whatever He shall hear, that shall He speak; and He will show
you things to come" John 16:13.

RESIST

Recognizing
Enemy
Spirit
Invoking
Spiritual
Truth

According to Webster, to resist is to oppose; to withstand; to strive against. The Word of God teaches us to resist the devil and he will flee from us.

"Submit yourselves, therefore to God. Resist the devil, and he will flee from you" James 4:7.

We must first identify our opposition before we can resist.

"Be sober, be vigilant, because your adversary, the devil, like a roaring lion walketh about, seeking whom he may devour; whom resist steadfastly in the faith" I Peter 5:7-8.

"The thief cometh not but to steal, and to kill, and to destroy; I am come that they might have life, and that they might have it more abundantly" John 10:10.

Once the opposition is identified, a plan of action must be put in place to overcome the adversary.

The believer draws his strength from his relationship with God who created heaven and earth. Our relationship with God equips us with special power in the form of His Word to deal with the enemy of our soul. When God's Word proceeds out of the mouth of a believer, it represents power-packed spiritual truth that allows him to resist the devil and put him to flight. The devil is no match for the Word of God.

"And they overcame him by the blood of the Lamb, and by the word of their testimony; and they loved not their lives unto the death" Revelation 12:11.

We must use the same strategy Jesus used when dealing with the devil. We must remind the devil continually that God's Word, representing spiritual truth and power, is our refuge and our strength.

We can resist the enemy once we have recognized and identified him and his strategies. God's Word, is full of spiritual truths and is available. It should be used to resist the enemy of our soul at all times.

REWARD

Righteous
Endeavors
Will
Always
Reap
Dividends

"But seek you first the Kingdom of God, and His righteousness; and all these things shall be added unto you" Matthew 6:33.

This scripture outlines God's condition for blessings and reminds us that His interest must always remain first.

"Let them shout for joy, and be glad, who favor my righteous cause: yea let them say continually, let the Lord be magnified, who has pleasure in the prosperity of His servant" Psalms 35:27.

What is His righteous cause? Could it be that it is outlined in Mark chapter 12?

"And Jesus answered him, the first of all the commandments is, Hear O Israel; the Lord our God is one Lord. And you shall love the Lord your God with all your heart, and with all your soul, and with all your mind, and with all your strength: this is the first Commandment. And the second is like namely this, you shall love your neighbor as yourself; there is none other commandment greater than these" Mark 12:29-31.

We can readily see that if we truly love God and our neighbor as our self, the answer to all of our problems will become very visible to us. War, prejudice, hatred, racism, jealously, envy, strife, etc. would cease to be.

God desires to reward His children. We are entitled to all His rewards as children of a loving and jealous God when we learn to walk in a righteous manner.

"If ye abide in me, and my words abide in you, ye shall ask what ye will, and it shall be done unto you" John 15:7.

RIGHTEOUSNESS

Revisiting
Inspired
God
Honored
Truths
Everytime
Our
Unbelief
Surfaces
Neutralizing
Enemy's
Sneaky
Surprises

We must conduct our lives in a manner that lines up with God's Word to be deemed righteous in His eyes. To remain righteous is an on going process. We must continually confess our sins and shortcomings to Him so that we can be cleansed from all our unrighteousness.

"If we confess our sins, He is faithful and just to forgive us our sin, and to cleanse us from all unrighteousness" I John 1:9.

Righteousness could be defined as a right standing with God. Our right standing with God is a result of our relationship with His Son, Jesus Christ. He redeemed us from the curse of the law and through grace brings us into the very presence of our Heavenly Father.

"But of Him are ye in Christ Jesus, who of God is made unto us wisdom, and righteousness, and sanctification, and redemption" I Corinthians 1:30.

We must revisit those inspired God-honored truths found in the Word of God every time unbelief surfaces. Staying connected to God through His Word allows us to live an overcoming life. The blood of Jesus applied to the life of the believer allows God to see us as righteous in His sight.

As David of old said in Psalms 119:11, *"Thy Word have I hidden in my heart, that I might not sin against thee."*

RISEN

Rightfully
Identifies
Savior's
Eternal
Nature

Jesus came into the world in the form of man to set the stage for identifying His eternal nature.

"And no man hath ascended into heaven, but He that came down from heaven, even the Son of man who is in heaven" John 3:13.

"That whosoever believeth in Him should not perish, but have everlasting life" John 3:15.

We are God's creation and are given the opportunity to be partakers of His divine nature. This is a result of His love for man that He expressed through the birth, death and resurrection of his Son, Jesus Christ.

"By which are given unto us exceeding great and precious promises, that by these ye might be partakers of the divine nature, having escaped the corruption that is in the world through lust" II Peter 1:4.

The fact that Christ was raised from the dead is proof positive that He is the Son of the living God.

"Saying, the Son of man must be delivered into the hands of sinful men, and be crucified, and the third day rise again" Luke 24:7.

"For in that He died, He died unto sin once; but in that He liveth, He liveth unto God" Romans 6:10.

Christ gave new meaning to death and hope for the believer.

"For the wages of sin is death, but the gift of God is eternal life through Jesus Christ our Lord" Romans 6:23.

A renewed relationship with the Heavenly Father resulted from His Son's willingness to give so that we could receive.

We walk in newness of life when we die out to self and allow our spirit to come alive.

"Therefore we are buried with Him in death, that as Christ was raised from the dead by glory of the Father, even so we should walk in the newness of life" Romans 6:4.

SALVATION

Son
Always
Lived
Viewing
Appointed
Time
Involving
Our
Need

As soon as Adam sinned God's master plan for man was placed into motion for man's redemption. In the 8th Century B. C. the prophet Isaiah wrote of the coming of Jesus the Son of God.

"For unto us a child is born, unto us a Son is given, and the government shall be on His shoulders; and His name shall be called Wonderful, Counselor, The Mighty God, The Everlasting Father, The Prince of Peace" Isaiah 9:6.

"Therefore the Lord himself shall give you a sign; Behold, the virgin shall conceive, and bear a Son, and shall call his name Immanuel" Isaiah 7:14.

Jesus took His assignment seriously and at the age of 12, He went with His parents to Jerusalem for the feast of the Passover. After the feast, His parents and the party that they were with began their trip home. After a day's journey, His parents realized Jesus was not with them so they returned to Jerusalem in search of Him. Three days later they found Him in the temple, sitting in the midst of the teachers, both hearing them and asking them questions. When questioned by His mother as to why He stayed behind, He responded with the answer that He must be about His master's business. (Luke 6:49)

At the age of 30 He had been fully prepared for service. He had proved that as the Son of God, He could occupy a physical body and live in world of sin and do so without sinning.

"For we have not an high priest who cannot be touched with the feelings of our infirmities, but was in all points tempted like as we are, yet without sin" Hebrews 4:15.

Jesus foretells his death in Luke 9:22

"Saying, the Son of man must suffer many things, and be rejected by the elders and the chief priests and scribes, and be slain, and be raised the third day."

Jesus was well aware of His assignment and appointed time involving man's need of salvation.

"For God sent not His Son into the world to condemn the world, but the world through Him might be saved" John 3:17.

SHADOW

Shows
Him
As
Divine
Overcoming
Word

A shadow, as defined by Webster, is an inseparable companion. The spirit of man cannot be seen but it is ever present wherever he may go. The wind, like the spirit of man, cannot be seen, however its affects can be seen.

A shadow can be seen with the natural eye, but it only represents an image of something real.

"Insomuch they brought forth the sick from the streets, and laid them on beds and couches, that at least the shadow of Peter passing by might overshadow some of them" Acts 5:15.

The shadow of Peter was his inseparable companion and served as an extension of himself and the anointing on his life.

Shadows take on varying shapes and sizes. A shadow needs the help of light and an object for its presence to appear. When we abide in the shadow of the Almighty we are walking in the light of God's Word, our inseparable companion.

"If ye abide in me, and my words abide in you, ye can ask what ye will, and it shall be done unto you" John 15:7.

"He that dwelleth in the secret place of the Most High shall abide under the shadow of the Almighty" Psalms 91:1.

When we learn to abide in Christ and His Word abide in us, then the light of the Word will direct our path and remove any shadow of doubt.

"And they overcame him by the blood of the Lamb, and by the word of their testimony; and they loved not their lives unto the death" Revelation 12:11.

SHEEP

Special
Hearing
Exposes
Enemy's
Plan

The enemy's plan is to steal, kill and destroy the sheep.

"The thief cometh not, but for to steal, and to kill, and to destroy: I am come that they might have life, and that they might have it more abundantly." John 10:10.

God, however, equipped the sheep of His flock with a special hearing that allows them to differentiate between an imposter and the Shepherd's voice.

God's sheep know His voice and the voice of a stranger they will not follow.

"And when he putteth forth his own sheep, he goeth before them, and the sheep follow him: for they know his voice. And a stranger will they not follow, but will flee from him: for they know not the voice of strangers" John 10:4-5.

"I am the good shepherd and know my sheep, and am known of mine." John 10:14.

Our shepherd is the Lord Jesus Christ.

"The Lord is my shepherd; I shall not want" Psalms 23:1.

The good Shepherd giveth His life for His sheep.

"I am the good shepherd; the good shepherd giveth his life for the sheep" John 10:11.

God alerts us to the fact that there are those who disguise themselves as shepherds but are no more than greedy dogs.

"Yea they are greedy dogs that can never have enough, and they are shepherds that cannot understand; they all look to their own way, every one for his gain, from his quarter" Isaiah 56:11.

"Woe be unto the pastors that destroy and scatter the sheep of my pasture! saith the Lord. Therefore thus saith the Lord God of Israel against the pastors that feed my people; Ye have scattered my flock and driven them away, and have not visited them: behold I will visit upon you the evil of your doings, saith the Lord" Jeremiah 23:1-2.

Followers of Christ are equipped with a shepherd's heart like that of Jesus.

"And I will give you pastors according to mine heart, which shall feed you with knowledge and understanding." Jeremiah 3:15.

"He shall feed his flock like a shepherd: He shall gather the lambs with His arm, and carry them in His bosom, and shall gently lead those that are with young" Isaiah 40:11.

A born again believer is equipped with the ability to hear the voice of the Good Shepherd and to be led by it. We must always remember that when we stray, we can come safely back in the fold of the Lord Jesus Christ by listening to His voice and following after it.

SPIRIT

Savior's
Presence
Is
Resident
In
Truth

We need to position ourselves each day to allow the Word of God to lead and guide us into all truths.

"Nevertheless, when He the Spirit of truth is come, He will guide you into all truths; for He shall not speak of Himself, but whatever He shall hear that shall He speak; and He will show you things to come" John 16:13.

We know that God is a spirit and that we must worship him in spirit and in truth.

"God is a spirit: and they that worship Him must worship Him in spirit and in truth" John 4:24.

The spirit of God comes alive in us at salvation and takes up residence in our heart. At this point, the birth of the spirit man creates an eternal connection with the Heavenly Father. We now have access to God through His Son, Jesus Christ for our every need.

The spirit of God comes into our life and takes up residence, desiring to remain as a permanent resident.

TOUCH

Thing
One
Uses
Connecting
Him

According to Webster, a trait is a stroke, hence, a touch. The relationship or connection that man has with God began in creation.

"And the Lord, God formed man of the dust of the ground, and breathed into his nostrils the breath of life; and man became a living soul" Genesis 2:7.

This was the initial divine touch or connection God had with man.

A connection with the Father through His Son, Jesus Christ is not limited by a distance barrier. When Jesus was approached by the centurion on behalf of a servant at home sick of the palsy, he stated, "I will come and heal him." The centurion replied, "Speak the word only and my servant shall be healed."

"And Jesus said unto the centurion, Go thy way; and as thou hast believed, so be it done unto thee. And his servant was healed in the selfsame hour" Matthew 8:13.

The connection here was one of conversation or with words. Jesus possessed the power to use words to change situations and circumstances because He was the living Word.

The woman with the issue of blood for 12 years made the statement if I can but touch the hem of His garment, I will be made whole. She had spent all that she had on physicians seeking a cure. She exercised her faith by touching the hem of His garment and was immediately made whole.

"But Jesus turned Him about and when He saw her, He said, Daughter, be of good comfort; thy faith hath made thee whole. And the woman was made whole from that hour" Matthew 9:22.

This connection resulted from a physical touch.

Every believer is blessed with the opportunity to go straight to the Throne of Grace through Jesus Christ and connect to the Father for every need they may have.

WARRIOR

Whole
Armor
Reveals
Readiness
In
Our
Relationship

Webster described a warrior as one who is experienced in or inclined to war; warlike; brave. A warrior in the army of God must be brave, courageous, and determined to fight for the cause of Christ.

The warrior taps into the resource of God's power through effective communication with the Father through prayer. Prayer will change situations and circumstances in our lives.

"Praying always with all prayer and supplication in the Spirit, and watching thereunto with all perseverance and supplication for all the saints" Ephesians 6:18.

The Word of God coupled with the Holy Spirit provides the warrior with needed strength to fight the good fight of faith.

"My son attend to my words; incline thine ear to my sayings. Let them not depart from thine eyes; keep them in the midst of thine heart. For they are life unto those that find them and health to all their flesh" Proverbs 4:20-22.

As a warrior in the Army of God we must study His Word until his mysteries become realities. God's Word is the single most powerful force in the universe. His Word is very clear about our position as a believer.

"If God be for us, who can be against us" Romans 8:31.

As we read further in the Romans 8, we see that the believer (warrior) is more that a conqueror.

"Nay in all these things, we are more than conquerors through Him that loved us. For I am persuaded that neither death, nor life, nor angels, nor principalities, nor powers, nor things present, nor things to come, nor height, nor depth, nor any other creation, shall be able to separate us from the love of God, which is in Christ Jesus or Lord" Romans 8:37-39.

As a warrior in the Army of God we are positioned to have angels on assignment at our beck and call.

"But to which of the angels said He at any time, Sit on my right hand, until I make thine enemies thy footstool? Are they not all ministering spirits, sent forth to minister for them who shall be heirs of salvation" Hebrews 1:13-14.

We must equip ourselves as warriors in the Army of God with the whole armor of God; knowing that we are more that conquerors because of our connection to the power source, God Himself. We must always be dressed in the whole armor of God and ready for battle against a formidable foe, Satan himself

WISDOM

Walking
In
Steps
Directed
Of
Master

"And many people shall go and say, Come ye, and let us go up to the mountain of the Lord, to the house of the God of Jacob; and He will teach us His ways, and we will walk in His paths; for out of Zion shall go forth the law, and the word of the Lord from Jerusalem" Isaiah 2:3.

"If any of you lack wisdom, let him ask of God, that giveth to all men liberally, and upbraideth not; and it shall be given him" James 1:5.

"I will instruct thee and teach thee in the way which thou shalt go: I will guide thee with mine eye" Psalms 32:8.

"For God giveth to a man that is good in His sight wisdom, and knowledge, and joy; but to the sinner He giveth travail, to gather and to heap up, that He may give to him that is good before God. This also is vanity and vexation of spirit" Ecclesiastes 2:26.

"Then shalt thou understand the fear of the Lord, and find the knowledge of God. For the Lord giveth wisdom: out of His mouth cometh knowledge and understanding. He layeth up sound wisdom for the righteous; He is a shield to those who walk uprightly" Proverbs 2:5-7.

When we focus our eyes on the Lord, He will teach us His ways that will enable us to walk in His paths. The wisdom of God is a gift from Him; it is ours for the asking.

God layeth up sound wisdom for the righteous for they are His children. Godly wisdom will help one to live an overcoming life and shield him from the devil and his craftiness. On the other hand, the wisdom of the world can be traced back to its roots, the devil himself. We cannot allow ourselves to get caught up in the wisdom of the world. We must keep our eyes focused on God and He will direct our paths.

WISE

Walking
In
Spirit
Everyday

Wise, according to Webster, is having the ability to form true judgment; discerning. We must learn to walk in the spirit everyday to be prepared to deal with the deceiver, Satan himself.

"And thou shalt take no bribe: for the bribe blindeth the wise and perverteth the words of the righteous" Exodus 23:8.

Everything must have a beginning and a foundation and wisdom is not exempted. The fear of God identifies each of us as possessing wisdom.

"The fear of the Lord is the beginning of wisdom. A good understanding have all that do His commandments; His praise endureth forever" Psalms 111:10.

Wise men find it necessary to walk in the Spirit of God so that their understanding is not distorted. God's ways are not our ways, nor His thoughts as our thoughts. This makes it necessary for us to remain in contact with Him at all times.

"But there is a spirit in man; and the inspiration of the Almighty giveth them understanding. Great men are not always wise; neither does the aged understand justice. Therefore I said, Hearken to me; I also will show mine opinion" Job 32:8-10.

God's opinion does matter.

Wise men will put their trust in God to direct their every footstep.

"Trust in the Lord with all thine heart and lean not to thine own understanding. In all thy ways acknowledge Him, and He shall direct thy paths. Be not wise in thine own eyes; fear the Lord and depart from evil" Proverbs 3:5-7.

Wise men recognize the cross as representing the power of God.

"For the preaching of the cross is to them that perish foolishness; but unto us who are saved it the power of God" I Corinthians 1:18.

Wise men walk in the spirit of God everyday.

When we learn to walk in the Spirit everyday, the Spirit will deliver us from our old nature thus producing righteousness.

"There is, therefore now no condemnation to them who are in Christ Jesus, who walk not after the flesh, but after the Spirit" Romans 8:1.

WOMAN

Willful
Obedience
Mastered
Adam
Nature

We are quick to blame Eve, the first woman, for the failure of man that brought sin into our environment. The devil thought his ability to deceive Eve would prove to be the crowning blow for all mankind. He failed to realize that an all-knowing God already had a master plan in place that would reunite mankind with God. The irony of it all was that the devil used woman as an instrument to separate us from God and God used woman to bring man back into a personal relationship with Him.

Mary's obedience to God's plan for her life is recorded in the first chapter of Luke's gospel. When approached by an angel of the Lord informing her that she had found favor with God and would conceive in her womb and bring forth a son she was to call Jesus, she was a bit confused. She asked the question how can this be seeing I know not a man? The angel of the Lord answered and said unto her that the Holy Spirit shall come upon thee, and the power of the Highest shall overshadow thee.
Her response was one of complete obedience when she answered the angel, be it unto me according to thy word.

The obedience by Mary, the mother of Jesus, provided man with the answer of how to deal with sin. The birth, death, burial and resurrection of her son would prove to be the answer to man's sin problem. The blood of Jesus was the supreme sin offering.

"Whom God hath set forth to be a propitiation through faith in His blood, to declare His righteousness for the remissions of sins that are past, through the forbearance of God" Romans 3:25.

"Much more then, being now justified by His blood, we shall be saved from wrath through Him" Romans 5:19.

"In whom we have redemption through His blood, even the forgiveness of sins;" Colossians 1:14.

"In whom we have redemption through His blood, the forgiveness of sins, according to the riches of His grace" Ephesians 1:7.

God's master plan proved to be more than a match for the devil. Man was now equipped with an antidote for sin, the blood of Jesus. This was all a result of Mary's obedience to God's plan for her life.

WORD

World's
Only
Real
Direction

Man has been in search of real direction since Adam disobeyed God in the Garden of Eden. Man's ability to cope with this problem was limited until the birth, death and resurrection of God's Son, Jesus Christ.

Satan used his deceptive power to convince Eve that she would possess godly power if she ate of the tree of knowledge of good and evil. Satan failed to tell the whole story. Eve did not take into consideration the fact that mankind was equipped only to deal with the good and not the evil side of man. This act of disobedience separated man from God. The separation remained in place until the arrival of Jesus Christ. Christ's obedience to His Father's plan even to the death on the cross provided redemption for man from sin.

The Word is the most important element in the life of a Christian. We take on the character of Jesus when we allow the Word to come alive in us. The Word engrafted into the spirit of man equips him to receive and enjoy the fruit of the Spirit. The flesh man becomes subject to the spirit man allowing the fruit to be present in our lives.

"But the fruit of the Spirit is love, joy, peace, long suffering, gentleness, goodness, faith, meekness, self-control, against such there is no law" Galatians 5:22-23.

The existence of the Word of God provides the basis for our faith. We are comforted in knowing that God's Word has been tested and tried and has never failed. God has said it and He will do it. What He has spoken He will make good. We can be confident in our daily walk because the steps of good man are ordered by God. We cannot allow ourselves to focus on man's ability to meet our every need because he not capable of doing so.

The Word of God is the only infallible truth.

"God is not a man, that He should lie; neither the son of man that he should repent: had He said, and shall not he do it? Or has he spoken, and shall He not make it good" Numbers 23:19.

Because the Word is eternal in duration this infallible truth cannot be changed.

"Jesus Christ the same yesterday, today, and forever" Hebrews 13:8.

The eternal duration of God's Word is defined for us in the book of Matthew.

"Heaven and earth shall pass away, but my words shall not pass away" Matthew 24:35.

God's Word is man's only real direction.

"Your Word is a lamp unto my feet and light unto my path" Psalms 119:105.

WORSHIP

Wholly
Obedient
Righteously
Serving
Him
In
Praise

Worship allows one to express his inner most feelings in an open manner toward his God.

"Let the word of Christ dwell in you richly, in all wisdom teaching and admonishing one another, in psalms and hymns and spiritual songs with grace in your hearts to the Lord" Colossians 3:16.

"Speaking to yourselves in psalms and hymns and spiritual songs, singing and making melody in your heart to the Lord" Ephesians 5:19.

We use praise and worship to get into the very presence of God.

"By Him, therefore, let us offer the sacrifice of praise to God continually, that is, the fruit of our lips giving thanks to His name" Hebrews 13:15.

"I will bless the Lord at all times; His praise shall continually in my mouth" Psalms 34:1.

Praise and worship causes God to focus His full attention on us.

"The eyes of the Lord are upon the righteous and his ears are open unto their cry" Psalms 34:15.

Once His attention is focused on each of us then we become the recipients of His blessings.

"The righteous cry, and the Lord heareth and delivereth them out of all their troubles" Psalms 34:17.

Worship is a way we express our love of God.

"Make a joyful noise unto God, all ye lands: sing forth the honour of His name: make His praise glorious" Psalms 66:1-2.

"Praise ye the Lord; for it is good to sing praise to our God; for it is pleasant; and praise is comely" Psalms 147:1.

YES

Yielding
Engages
Supernatural

We position ourselves to be recipients of God's abundant blessings when we learn to say yes to His call to service.

"With good will doing service, as to the Lord, and not to men: Knowing that whatsoever good thing any man does; the same shall he receive of the Lord, whether he be bond or free" Ephesians 6:7-8.

"Now be ye not stiffnecked as your fathers were, but yield yourselves unto the Lord, and enter into the Sanctuary, which He has sanctified forever: and serve the Lord your God, that the fierceness of His wrath turn away from you" II Chronicles 30:8.

"Neither yield you your members as instruments of unrighteousness unto sin: but yield yourselves unto God, as those who are alive from the dead, and your members as instruments of righteousness unto God. For sin shall not have dominion over you: for you are not under the Law, but under Grace. Know you not that to whom you yield yourselves servants to obey, his servants you are to whom you obey; whether of sin unto death, or of obedience unto righteousness" Romans 6:13-16.

Yielding ourselves unto God is another way of saying yes to God and becoming instruments of righteousness. We must always remember that yielding is a continuing process that we must remain engaged in. It cannot be practiced as an on- today/off-tomorrow process or it will be of little benefit to the believer. We have tapped into the source of power for controlling our Adamic nature when we learn to say yes to God's plan for our lives.

About the Author

At a very young age, I accepted Jesus Christ into my heart as my personal savior. My walk with God spans some sixty years. I have always looked to His Word as a lamp unto my feet and a light unto my path.

Through the years, I have served in many areas, from a youth Sunday School teacher, adult Sunday School teacher, Sunday School Superintendent, board member, and in prison ministry.

My walk with God has helped me to see and experience the value of the Word of God in the life of a believer. It falls right in line with my life purpose statement taken from Proverbs 4:20-22.

I will attend to the Word of God by inclining my ears to His sayings, and not letting them depart from my eyes. I will keep them in the midst of my heart for they are life and health to me.

www.ingramcontent.com/pod-product-compliance
Lightning Source LLC
Chambersburg PA
CBHW051813040426
42446CB00007B/652